Full Moon Boat

Also by Fred Marchant
Tipping Point

Full Moon Boat

Poems

Fred Marchant

Graywolf Press
Saint Paul, Minnesota

Publication of this volume is made possible in part by a grant provided by
the Minnesota State Arts Board through an appropriation by the Minnesota
State Legislature, and by a grant from the National Endowment for the Arts.
Significant support has also been provided by the Bush Foundation; Dayton's,
Mervyn's, and Target stores through the Dayton Hudson Foundation; the
McKnight Foundation; and other generous contributions from foundations,
corporations, and individuals. To these organizations and individuals we
offer our heartfelt thanks.

Published by Graywolf Press
2402 University Avenue, Suite 203
Saint Paul, Minnesota 55114
All rights reserved.

www.graywolfpress.org

Published in the United States of America

ISBN 1-55597-311-6

2   4   6   8   9   7   5   3   1
First Graywolf Printing, 2000

Library of Congress Catalog Card Number: 00-101776

Cover art: Gregory Amenoff, *Starry Floor IV,* 86″ X 64″, oil on canvas, 1994

Cover design: Jeanne Lee

Acknowledgments

Several of the poems in this book were originally published, sometimes in different form, in the following journals and anthologies. I wish to thank the editors for their encouragement.

AGNI: "Diana's Lamp," "Delphi," "Rows of Buddhas, Receding"
America: "Ensemble"
The Antigonish Review: "Bubble Net"
The Boston Review: "Letter"
College English: "Archives"
Compost: "The Tea Stall," "The River Guard"
Harvard Magazine: "Owning"
Harvard Review: "Fragments on the Last Night," "Seven Tongues of God"
The Journal: "Wax"
Lingo: "Trestle at Mystic"
Meanie: "Octane"
Orion: "Thereinafter"
Peacework: "Thirty Obligatory Bows"
Persephone: "Harpagus"
Ploughshares: "Corita's Tank"
Salamander: "Glassblower's Apprentice," "Winter Range," "27 Down, Meaning *Deep Sleep*," "The Vole," "The Frog"
Southern Humanities Review: "Providence, Halfway," "Estuary, iv."
Tampa Review: "Bones to Hà Nội," "Estuary, ii."
Văn Nghệ (Hà Nội): "Inscription," translated into Vietnamese by Nguyễn Quang Thiều
Venture: "Readies to Fall," "The Kinh Thầy Ferry"
Web del Sol: "Inscription," "The Visitor"
Weber Studies: "Estuary, iii."

"Letter" also appeared in *Mountain River,* edited by Kevin Bowen, Nguyễn Bá Chung, and Bruce Weigl, published by the University of Massachusetts Press, 1998.

"Screen Porch" appeared in *Urban Nature,* edited by Laure-Anne Bosselaar, published by Milkweed Editions, 2000.

"Archives" and "Hué, in Darkness" appeared in *Winners: A Retrospective of the Washington Prize,* edited by Karren Alenier, Hilary Tham, and Miles Moore, published by The Word Works, 2000.

"The Alabaster Stork" appeared in *Writing Between the Lines,* edited by Kevin Bowen and Bruce Weigl, published by the University of Massachusetts Press, 1997.

I want to thank Fiona McCrae, Anne Czarniecki, Janna Rademacher, Jeff Shotts, and all the other members of the staff at Graywolf Press. Their editorial patience, imagination, and faith have been invaluable. In addition, many friends have read and commented on poems in this book as they have evolved. I feel deep gratitude to all of those readers, and wish to thank especially the following: Jenny Barber, Kevin Bowen, Jane Brox, Andrea Hollander Budy, Bob Clawson, Bill Corbett, Martha Collins, Eamon Grennan, Lola Haskins, Jonathan Holden, Askold Melnyczuk, Nguyễn Bá Chung, David Rivard, Stefi Rubin, Trần Đăng Khoa, and Bruce Weigl.

for Stefi, always

Contents

For a country without a past is nothing, a word
That, hardly spoken, loses its meaning.

—Czesław Miłosz, "A Legend," 1949

I

The Return

When he poured acid for his etching,
Blake said the art he practiced was infernal,
meaning it brimmed with the energy of demons
who first of all had been angels. On the wall
of the bedroom I inherited from my grandfather
hung a gold-framed etching titled "The Return"—
a doughboy kneeling before a larger-than-life
crucifix, the helmet and rifle on the floor,
his calves wrapped with puttees, his head
half-hidden by a bulging, cinched-up knapsack.

Harry, older uncle on my mother's side,
quit college to go to France in 1916.
He flew a Spad in the Lafayette Escadrille,
and never wanted to fly again afterwards.
In one photo the polished sash of his Sam
Browne belt gleams in the ocean sunlight.
He is sailing home, and a swell has leaned
him into the bulkhead. Under the smile
you can see his fear that life thereafter
would turn out to be another flying coffin.

In 1970, Georgette, Harry's war bride,
wrote to me on Okinawa, pleading that
I not leave the service as a conscientious
objector. She said Jesus could not approve,
He had smiled on America, and I owed
back some portion of what I had been given.
The airplane I flew home on, my c.o.
discharge in hand, was an empty, airborne
auditorium, another sign of the nation's excesses.
When I woke, I looked out over the desert,

and at first I thought I saw a land split
apart by our history of rage and sorrow,
but as we cruised through a vast clarity
of air thousands of feet up, the creases
of deep, dried-out arroyos reminded me
of the pack that belonged to the soldier
who hung over my childhood sleep
and taught me, before I ever understood
a word like puttee, how good it would feel
to take a helmet off, set the weapon down.

Wax

My mother coming to me, trying to comfort.
But am I the child crying? Is she coming *for*?

Her terrible fearsweat.

A moat of summer night, circle of innocence,
All the world's windows wide open, crying.

All ears, I,

And sanctuary while a car, whose headlights swing
Across the room, stops, idles.

She is crying.

All ears the maples and elms, the pointy leaves sifting her whispers.
And then me too.

Me too in the afterstorm,

"Don't worry," I say, but we worry,
We worry like candles wavering, alert, spilling,

All the long blue night.

The Vole

Meaning with its pines
and willows, tamed hillsides,

and mother's mouth-stories of glaciers
passing like dream-time beasts

sculpting the earth and leaving behind
such rock as to shore up our house,

the layers I find as I dig below
my first hole. Milkpod

and timothy stretch ahead like
an impossible number of days,

so far into the future
a red-tailed hawk, wings unmoving

and circling a panic of *yes,*
can hear the small pleading of the I.

Am here, says I, now come.

Octane

I began in the realm of engine
and lit workbench, down among
unsorted screws, nuts, and washers,
next to a monkey wrench and ballpeen
hammer, with ratchets, and a vise grip,
its teeth broken, the bar shiny from use.
I climbed among black horns of radiator
hoses, and poked at discard batteries,
their acids bubbling from within.
I stood at attention by lit-up pumps,
those idols draped with red, plastic
pennants. Probed the iridescent gobs
of grease, breathed in a vivid, wavering
gasoline that wanted only a match,
longed to be radically other,
to be a flare of pure becoming, so bright
no one would know who else had been there,
whose hands had held and lifted me up.

The Frog

Ciborium—nuns—broad breastplates of starched radiance—
a soupspill at lunch—an orange dot of need—my desire
to touch—the crisp cloth would hum like a tuning fork—
the frog—hidden in a fold—a clicker painted green—
metal flap for the belly—one click to stand—two to sit—
oaken pews smoothed by the spines curved into them—
tingly sweetness of incense—the priest's arms uplifted
and roping the light—the Paschal candle tall as a man—
creamy yellow—wax pooling and ready to spill—three clicks—
cool in the dark—we alcoved lambs—high heels tapping
to the rail—worn heels—seamed nylon calves—wrinkles on
the cloth—the body imposed, imposing—always the bottom—
the underneath, the creases—a nun who swirled in silence—
cat's-paw crepe of her soles—four clicks—at the left ear—
the light of the world—on my knees again.

Readies to Fall

Child home, sick and happy, from school,
a winter day become a moss-covered rock in June,
him flipping it over into a humid afternoon indoors,
guarded by an icicle broadsword.

Sanguine the seminarians sleeping at the rectory.

Upright the altar boys, their surplices like tea cozies.
Introibo ad altare Dei
are the only words I remember, and a slap I got for forgetting,
then back to the pews, just one of the many.

What were the Twelve Sorrowful Mysteries?
What were the Joyful?

Isn't the image you hold in your mind when you pass
that which you will come back as?
There were trolley wires coated by a sleet-riddled storm.
Electric-blue sparks in bursts.

And a relieved glint on the icicle, as it readies to fall.

Glassblower's Apprentice

Turn of the last century,
and him awkward as a colt.

The compound molten,
glistening with demand,

the pipe sooty to his lip.
He relinquishes,

saying he is all thumbs.
He is told by the master

that
is explanation, not excuse.

At the end of his vision—
the green life awaits,

the clear new world to come
burning like a star.

He is ordered,
You must not breathe,

lest he scorch his lungs,
but he is entranced, eager,

greedy to get started,
to be one of us.

So he does.
In.

Diana's Lamp

An ivory slide rule left me by my grandfather
became a measuring wand, my prophet and sign
of bent-over-a-hairline calibrations of the real.

He was waked in the living room. A priest
intoned a full rosary above him, and I was told
to stay put on the velvet chair, to be quiet

under a lamp made out of a cast of the goddess,
her bow in hand, a quiver of arrows on her back,
one breast out of her tunic. Trailed by whippets,

she walked under a curling brass vine, at the tip
of which was a bulb that shone with the same
thin light that falls now on the white pines

outside my window, and on the cords of cut timber
thickened by imagined elements of earth and heaven,
neither of which is the nature I long for anymore.

Trouble Light

I'll be right over,
my father shouted into the phone.
The greasy shirt he buttoned, his backing
out without looking told me it was another
break-in, that he would cross the city
to his station where the cops would be
waiting by the pumps, radios hissing,
a window smashed, the register jimmied,
cash drawer hanging out like a tongue.

Quick then to the lift, and the well underneath,
an overshoe he had hidden down there,
a fist-sized wad of cash in the toe. Under
the yellow trouble light in its wire cage,
he counted. Outside, in a dawn that looked
coughed up, he turned to the cop, a man
he did not know but for whom he now had
unbounded fellow-feeling, and whispered,
Still there, all there.

Night Swim, Lake Mishnock

I, shawled in a towel before her,
am ten.

I slap at the mosquitoes which have found
my calf, while she stubs out a menthol Kool,
and sends sparks flying.

Like the lightning bugs,
or the shore lights blinking over the silky water
I've just splashed out of.

Low, dim, downshifting truck sounds out on the highway.
I replay for her my long swim over the weeds
I thought wanted to pull me down.

A little shiver as I speak.

The radio on her porch has begun to play
my favorite song. It's about Betty Lou,
her new pair of shoes,
and the guy who loves her is so happy
he sings with the chorus, *Wah-ooh, wah-ooh*.

I am amazed at how much this makes me feel,
though I cannot tell what it is I'm feeling.
I know so little about sex,
I think it must be like swimming at night
and love, like reaching the shore.

I know just enough about both
to think I hear them in the song.

II

Screen Porch

Summer nights I loved the cool pillow
as it settled into dampness,

the city noise as it dwindled,
the smell of plants, lights in the apartment

across the street going out. Crickets.
First light had to be inferred from shadows

slipping off locusts, and tall wild sumacs,
from wet sparkles in the mesh,

a daddy longlegs looking right at you.

Tereus

How it was a passion.
How it felt like fury, but was desire.
How it was desire to debase,
which was desire to be felt deeper than flesh can feel.
How it began in blood, and ended with more.
How it was a stutter, a knotted rope writhing in the throat.
How it was fate rooting underneath,
and a tongue thrust toward the sun.
A bush that shuddered and called me out.
How the cave listened.
How her sounds,
quick and watery, took wing,
how blood could flow like speech.
How it thickened with curse and filled with knowledge
and bound me to her.
How I struck her with my fist.

African Violets

In the empty part of the afternoon,
    perhaps the hour between two and three,
a time when you sneak a nap,
when a deliveryman pulls his truck under a tree
    certain no one would know the difference.
For my mother it would be just before that driver
    got home, when there would be a time she would
        call free, and mean free enough to pour out
her suffering and worry.

How I hated to have to listen.
How I listened as hard as I could.
It was like having a constant sunburn, with her hand
    resting on it.

Betrayal, beatings, an abandonment,
    the nightly tray with whiskey and beer
my father carried up to his mother in our attic flat.
When he came down to eat his supper,
    he would be ready to fight. His mother would have said
        his wife needed "a talking to."
There would be bruises, a broken pair of glasses,
    and all the next day tears that seemed to ooze.

Here is the lesson about the nature of love:
    never swear at a woman, never raise my hand.
I don't remember what I said in return,
    I said so little.
I was pure listening in training,
I sat as far away from her as I could,
    the far end of the couch, and across the room
where a blond throw rug from China was between us.

It was next to the table with African violets,
    where I studied their leaves, deep purple petals,
        and bright yellow eyes at the heart.

It would be this time of day,
    when lemon-yellow light warms the rug
and feeds the indoor flowers that quiver whenever
    a car slows and sounds as if it will stop.
An hour when people who know each other
    better than they know themselves
murmur words that are truer in tone than meaning.

When simplicities of feeling are offered as promises,
    gifts are accepted, and lessons learned,
        no matter how much they hurt.

The Pale

You want to give me credit for being
unlike where we came from, neither
planed nor patted down. . .

but I, standing in front of your students
try to explain. My mother was divorced
and remarried, and thus

excommunicated, "denied the sacraments."
This made me, spiritually, a parish ward,
"a little bastard,"

according to the pious Father Prime,
who said it was a good lesson to learn
about the nature of sin.

So it was not the same as with you,
not skin color, but more an eddy of barely
perceptible distress,

which swirled round us whenever we knelt,
palms together, tongues lifted, eyes shut,
elbows on the rail.

I remember our blue ties askew,
our shirttails wandering up from our belts,
and both of us somehow already beyond.

Mes Amis

Brother Cyril, his cheeks
beet-red with ire at the "hooligans,"

the quaintness of his word
another sign of the dimming

of his signal. He spoke a pursed,
cut-crystal French,

our "vocabs" and the declension
of irregular verbs floating

like chalk dust as he paced the length
of the blackboard and steadied himself,

while we made gestures—
thumb in the open mouth—

to mean he had been drinking again.
Or held our noses,

because he stunk of the Aqua Velva
he had slapped on to cover the whiskey lunch.

All winter the steam would pulse
through pipes deep in that red-brick building.

If we had been better or older
we might have imagined the knocking

was his heart dying to get out,
but to our eyes he was neither brother

nor father, but only old, celibate,
and teaching what we would never use.

Nothing could save him.

Providence, Halfway

I'd like to wake at sea, rise at dawn and paint
the disappearing night fog—shades of white
for the fog, shades of black for the rest.

I would resist thinking these had anything to do
with race, or the memory of a morning centered
on me and Eddie Bolden, on different sides

of a rusted fence, him black, me white, and neither
of us much beyond six, grasses up to our thighs,
as we spoke about what I cannot recall,

but am certain was not a reason to punch me
in the face, which he wound up and did anyway.
Was I bragging about my clothes, the yard?

Or was it a tone that he alone could hear,
one that said I thought the world was good,
or would be, at least to me. Something about

my easy smile under fair-weather clouds
and shade catalpas where neighborhoods
abutted, the corner of Camp Street and Locust,

halfway up the hill to Hope and some other
names for irony that have washed ashore
here in Providence and its adjacent Plantations.

Owning

The great joy of it,
the red and green brilliance,

the parrot that it is,
most surely is, one horny leg

curling a claw into
the corner of an otherwise

articulate mouth,
its wrapping itself around

words those of you
who own nothing at all

cannot imagine
the likes of: papers *passed,*

titles *claimed.*
It inks all the records

with a deep green plume
and bloody little tip.

Trestle at Mystic

Region of wreckage: a barge
      vivid with rot,
low tide, muck. Friable soil

on the gull-dotted landfill.
      Beside the tracks,
a pair of cops climb down

from a Jeep, as if looking
      for evidence
at the edge of a forest

of swaying sumac and cattail.
      Shanties of
plywood, old doors, sawhorses.

A clothesline hung with sheets,
      underwear,
and the other flags of those

who live here where a trestle
      slows the train
and I behind papers and a window

am trying to read the language
      of a carnival
of names spray-painted

over bolted girders forged
      in Bethlehem,
"The Birth Place of Steel."

The Alabaster Stork

by Trần Đăng Khoa
co-translated with Nguyễn Bá Chung

When rain blackens the sky in the east,
when rain blackens the sky in the west,
when rain blackens the sky in the south, the north,

I see a stork white as alabaster
take wing and usher in the rain. . .

Rice in the paddy will ripple like a broad flag.
Potato plants will unfold their darkened leaves,
and palm tree fronds will try to catch the drops.
Toads and frogs will sing all day and night.
The silver fins will be dancing to that tune.

But no one sees in the branches
the stork shivering in the cold. . .

When rain blackens again the sky in the east,
when rain blackens again the sky in the west,
when rain blackens again the sky in the south, the north,

I see that stork white as alabaster
take wing to proclaim the rain again.

Thirty Obligatory Bows

Television last night,
a smooth homage to Hotel Company, bleeding on Hill 881.
The remembered command to a private to retrieve another,
then two of them dead. The former lieutenant,

his high-pitched voice, his almost-tears,
the "human interest" in those tears, the announcer pausing.
My skin crawling in the easy chair.
A flying reel of relived arguments, distinctions,

then the spool out of control, film flapping away.
The lieutenant reporting he was spit on.
My wondering if I had to believe him.
My feeling mean-spirited at my wondering.

He owns the largest garden center in L.A.,
all that life under translucent plastic tenting,
From the steps of the pagoda where Thích Quảng Đúc
left to burn himself in Sài Gòn, I took a photograph

which centered on a dragon boat
drifting on the Perfume River, framed by a full-leafed
banana tree. An image of mourning.
Another photograph: this one in front of the Marine insignia,

my right hand raised, joining. I am flanked
by my parents, their eyes odd and empty too.
It was 1968, and none of us knew what we were doing.
Upstairs, over my desk hangs a plaque with horns

from a Vietnamese mountain deer.
At school I have a lacquer of a poet wearing spectacles,
squatting, writing with a brush.
He lives near the One Pillar Pagoda.

My shelves are crowded with the books I teach:
the anatomies of sorrow, almanacs and unit histories,
Time-Life photo collections, topographical maps,
all the explanations I will ever need.

Today my friend Tô Nhuận Vỹ
and his young daughter Diệu Linh are coming to visit.
She has never seen snow before, and kneels down,
touches it to her face, is surprised and delighted.

Now they are on the salted steps and I shout out
Be careful, it's very slippery here!
The words float in the freezing air. Thirty years since,
and everything's changed, but not utterly.

III

Archives

The photographs are kept in flint-gray boxes,
wheeled in on waist-high carts that squeak
and irritate the researcher taking notes nearby.
I lift the flimsy, protective tissue as if it were
gauze through which blood has been seeping,
and beneath is a field hospital where a medic
tends to a civilian woman's wounded hip.
His eyes say she's worse off than she thinks.

Next is a corpse in a hammering sun, torso
twisted over his legs. Squatting beside him
is a boy whose bare white arms rest lightly
on his knees, a cigarette in his cupped hand.
The asked-for smile floats on his face,
is embarrassed and loyal only to the dead.

Bones to Hà Nội

He is wary in the train station,
the rucksack bundled in his arms
as if it were holy. He tries to be
casual so as not to let anyone think
it is important enough to steal.
There is a policy which forbids
boarding a train with the remains
of a body, but surely others have
done so, even if the train would
then be haunted by an unburied
soul, and dangerous for a while.
But these are a brother's bones,
coming back from a ditch in
the South. Ten years and still
many are intact. Tibia, fibula,
digits, vertebrae. How can he
be sure he has them all or whose
are which? Pieces are scattered
at the bottom of the rucksack,
inside the curve of half-ribs
that fence his toiletries, a change
of clothing. Such packing makes
it very difficult to find his novel,
so he sits like a peasant to market,
leaning on what no one knows
he holds. He feels devoid of
thoughts other than suspicion,
and feels dry-hardened as these
he loves, carries, and cannot smell.

27 Down, Meaning *Deep Sleep*

Four letters, beginning with "C."

I am stung by the word's first meaning,
one I hadn't known until now, as the puzzle
dissolves into the Sunday afternoon
my father died, its downpour splashing
on the cement patio, the large clay pots,
the wrought-iron table painted gold.

From the living room of his senior citizen
housing, Matthew XXV, named after
the Gospel reference to "the least of you,"
I went to check on him in the bedroom.
He had been sleeping, but now his eyes
were open, and I could see he was still alive.
Only later did I learn the right word was
unresponsive—alive but not really there.
In a panicky twilight of what to do, I waited
a few more minutes, then called the Rescue.

I studied the bend in the glass straw
and wondered where he'd hidden his whiskey.
I remembered how much this man loved to sleep.
Loved its refuge, but also the honest bargain
between mind and labor, the latter rewarded
with ease by the god of ordinary trade,
a simple god he could believe in.
I hoped he was only dreaming.
I hoped the voices he heard belonged to those
he wanted to be among, that they would greet him
with delight when he woke.

Letter

by Trần Đăng Khoa
co-translated with Nguyễn Bá Chung

Mother, I may well fall in this war,
fall in the line of duty—as will so many others—
just like straw for the village thatch.
And one morning you may—as many others—
hold in your hand a piece of paper,
a flimsy little sheaf of paper
heavier than a thousand-pound bomb,
one that will destroy the years you have left.

Even so, don't weep. . . I'm not dead yet.
Why not read in the *Tale of Kiều?*
Maybe then, peace under the shade of our palm.
You could lean on the door and wait for me
as you used to. You could listen for our steps,
see us coming home from school, arm in arm,
laden with books, giggling by the window,
as the evening passes into silence.

When night settles over the house,
　　　　over the garden. . .
　　　　　　over the sky. . .
night warm and smooth as silk,
I want you to leave the door ajar.

Through the house a wind will sing
its love of sky and cloud, and bring you
to the sweet arms of sleep, unaware
your son has slipped in, found his way
home on airs that wander the earth
seeking only to soothe the mothers
whose children have been lost.

Harpagus

. . . for Astyages himself there were set tables of mutton, but, before Harpagus, the flesh of his own son, all save for the head and extremities of the hands and the feet; these were kept separate, covered up in a basket.

—Herodotus, *The History*

On the evening of the feasting
no matter where I looked I saw the deep golden weave
of watertight palm burnished with a light not its own.

Had Astyages asked,
I would have said forgiveness in his heart
had made greatness in his rule.
The wild god of my fear had withdrawn its claws,
and I felt free to tell how I had given Cyrus
as infant to the herdsman who in turn was to give
the child to the mountain.

I told what I remembered of the time:
I stood in the dark hut of the herdsman
and watched clouds speckle the hillside as he climbed
and disappeared into a narrow notch.
A bell sounded in the herd as I mourned the life
of the twisting bundle struggling like a bird.

Who could mistake the young man who stood now
before Astyages, his eyes intent upon a king
who praised the gods for thwarting his wishes?

When the king motioned for me, I thought
the basket might be an offering to the All-Seeing,
so I approached with equanimity.
When he asked me how I liked this feasting,
I said I had loved it as much as my life,
and when he pressed to know which dishes
in particular, I told him all but one.

No one knew whereof we spoke.
In his manner, no sign of cruelty.
I, who for a lifetime had held his trust,
took the basket to burn. I would not look inside
again, nor touch my son. I myself lit the fire
and breathed the smoke before it leapt onto the wind.
I wondered in what heart, in which breast,
this child so much the best of myself, would rest.

Windows

This is the window of the leapt,
oldest of all.
The dream of flight,
a quiver of desire at the edge,
the heart like a match struck.

And this, the window of the fallen,
easiest to open.
The embarrassment
of accident, a wedding ring
down the dark, mistaken drain.

This is the window of the pushed,
The didn't-know-what-hit-him
as he dropped,
the feathery nudge of the nation,
its high court of necessity.

And this, the window of the overheard,
the aftermath in the telephone:
"Well, he's gone,"
says one end of the wire to the other,
which replies, "That's too bad."

The Collage House

for Eric Olson

I crawled on my knees and glued magazine
photos to white construction paper.
You said it was controlled regression, essence
of all therapy. I must have felt like a child—
I placed an image of a newborn entering
the world at the center of my collage.

I surrounded him with various breasts,
circled them with scenes of war: the wounded
riding on armor, Hiroshima scenes, flimsies
of my discharge papers, a torn photo
of the street execution in Sài Gòn. The bland
indifference of one man, the grimace of the other.

You said mine was a collage of remarkable reason.
I said it looked like an asteroid belt.
You'd just finished reading a theorist on the floating
signifier and said each image was a particle
which would inevitably transform the other.
I said I sure hoped so. I still do.

Now, your father's coffin-liner hangs swaying
off the end of a backhoe, the body soon
to be uncased, and turned over
to the stainless-steel tray of autopsy.
The story to be given to the red light
of the documentary camera. A pathologist

stands in a lab coat and says he's "pretty sure"
the death they said was suicide in 1953
was neither a jump nor a fall.
You cannot help but wonder who hit him,
who muscled him up to a sill high in the Statler,
and gave him to the icy, whistling air.

The interviewer wants to know
if your effort to find out what had happened
was worth what it had cost you.
I see you standing at the rim of an enormous
canyon, the layers of earth lit up with sunlight.
A punishing trail leads to the bottom.

If there is a spirit in this place,
it calls you down to a river that runs
beneath all the lies. If only it could tell you
what it knows, if only there were a shoreline
where you could kneel and look deeply
into the images that river might bring you,

but there is no Collage House waiting—
no scissors, no paste, no mystery of the life
of the mind, no place for the story
the exhumed body will tell,
only a wilderness of ground glass and lye,
and the long struggle not to swallow it.

The Phoenix Program

Afterwards, the children stood outside
the house of their birth
to witness how it too had to be punished.

When they came of age, they fled to the capital,
lost themselves in the study of history and great works of art,
graduated in swirling, carmine robes.

Burdened with a knowledge that murderers
name their deeds after winged deities,
they dream for a while of claws on the back,

but later they become certain there was
nothing they could have done.
And they are not alone.

It is like this throughout the city.
On each corner you can see them—
leaning as if the vanishing point on their horizon

were other than ours.
They speak quietly only to one another.
They play no instruments, and do not sing.

Inscription

People ask you for lullabies.
They want you to blow dust off the roses.
They'll tell you your job is to imagine engines have hearts.
I think it is best to say nothing.
Tell it to no one. Be armor and sloth.
Tell them there is nothing more to be said.
Let them think you are dead.

IV

Delphi

i.

"I" —
the very use of that pronoun was what I had come to suspect.
I said, "Because being is but a solvent,
the ego is not separate from space or time, but one with them."

In the sun-slanted Gothic office, over the green, opened Loeb editions,
a splayed stack of geometric Greek,
my teacher said he felt he'd washed up on Nausicaä's island,
still agile, but wary, a relic from a more brutal age.

I said, "Mine would be a paper on the nature of the mystical vision
in the *Agamemnon*. . ."
He looked out at me from the entrance into the House of Atreus,
and said, "We all stand ankle deep in someone's blood."

". . . but with emphasis on Cassandra," I continued, "prisoner, lover, oracle,
swept into a no-time in which all time is present,
a no-place everywhere at once, a vision fastened on the moment of death,
which is the very nature of art."

"No," my teacher said, "her words are only what the wide, granite slabs
of the divine manage to press out of her."
I said, "But what she says is luminous, the essence of song."
"Sparrow," I called her,

"what the human mind could in duress become open to,
her own horrors notwithstanding. . . a lens of bright language. . .
the essence of poetry."
"One kind," he said, "and not mine."

ii.

He wanted poetry embedded in time,
in history, in earned truths of sequence,
that is to say, of syntax, slow and deliberate,
building the barrow stone by stone.
He craved too the base metal of irony,
its tacit image of a world in fracture.
Not the single vision, but signs of limits
on the human. A poetry of the day
after the peace has begun, when furies
have been talked back into the earth.
Not voices swept in with the whirlwind,
but those of the shelter, where whispered
kindnesses pass among those who survive,
who lie curled in the trunk of a hollow tree.

Thereinafter

crested, hungry—nowhere seen—only a pecking heard—
a hollow branch offered—a yielding bronze bell of memory—
log striker—words welling—like laughter, mostly unbidden

Seven Tongues of God

My first time, my friend said, nothing will change,
    everything will be the same, including myself,
        only more so.

I understood it to be what it is, an acid, an ergot derivative,
    a must, a blight on a rotten berry,
        a nausea in apparition,

but it feels like tripod molecules have landed on the moon,
    the cells applauding, while that marvel,
        the lacy architecture

of reason is melting to goose fat, to tendons and nerves
    with marrow-rich sockets of feeling
        which stretch out

like a sleek animal lodged under the skin. My heart is
    trotting like a tall horse under a tall rider,
        withers trembling

at the breeches and crop of aristocracy. The self I know
    has elided into the terrors of the dwarfed
        as it leaps the wall,

and crashes through leaves, stands stock-still, not
    even breathing. Shadows lick at
        its shoulders.

The cicadas sound like a cry for help, a plea for life,
    a life I have just begun to love,
        only more so.

Winter Range

new snow overnight—

　　　　　　　—dry, clean crystals

clouds when—

　　　　　　　—you step into them

cottonwood—

　　　　　　　—two eagles shift

their hoodlike wings—

　　　　　　　—talons deep, the bark frozen

a white hillside—

　　　　　　　—silence of a breath held

facing the sun—

　　　　　　　—a pulse in the ear saying

what little it could—

　　　　　　　—the little you could hear

Bubble Net

In a domain of pinion
and stridor, of blue heron,

and the cone of a mountain
gone crimson at sunset,

the herring at the surface
thrash, trapped in a ring

of bubbles, airy illusions,
while deep below a gaping

hungry humpback starts
to ascend. Who are you

to want what is less than
this, or other?

The Visitor

With a ceremonial hush,
a line of feeling comes to rest
on nothing more supple than
the mind of day, that leather-worker
with thickened fingers, that mechanic
whose spanner slips off the bolt.
Oh how we want to stay put
in the lilacs, like bees with bellies
covered in rich, velvety yellow.
We are certain the just-arrived
elegant one has no interest in us,
not us. He has unlatched the gate,
he has strolled past the plumeria,
and past the royal poinciana.
He stands now under the pillars
of the gleaming white portico,
at the far end of which we twist
on our wicker chairs and wonder
with our bodies, *Who could it be?*

A Reading during Time of War

It is the moment just before,
    with no intent to punish,

a wish for all to be air
    and scrubbed by rain,

filled with eagerness to learn
    and be if not a child

then openhearted, at ease,
    never to have heard

of the bending river
    that stretches to the delta

where a bloated corpse
    bumps softly,

snags on a tree stump
    and, waterlogged,

rolls slowly, just below.

Full Moon Boat

Yes, sell the compass, come on the boat of the full moon.
—Hồ Chí Minh, "Full Moon in January," 1948

i. Ensemble

When the drumhead's skin is tightened
just enough, and the zither with inlaid
pearl discovers the key,

when the vibrato spool of the đan-bầu
and the strings of the moon lute
find themselves,

when stick castanets and finger teacups
begin to shiver, and singers in carmine
silk begin their courting,

when a warm, steady rain starts to weep
over tiaras, and the back and forth
lean of planting,

then the northern lands will learn a river music,
and begin to flower.

ii. The River Guard

Tank-wallow,
moat of the mortared,
sap of cemeteries, their perfume bleeding
into waters steeped in sandalwood,

sweet vein of the Buddha we float on,
glistening pulse that scours the buffalo.
"This," says my friend leaning over the side,
". . . my Mother."

Of whom he lifts what he can, and drinks.

iii. The Tea Stall

We sit on worn, wobbly wooden stools.

Under a rusted corrugated roof,
heating in the midday sun
a pretty girl refills our cups.

She says she's not sure she'll ever marry,
and eyes the hired cars trying
to sneak onto the ferry,
the angry, red silk armband waving them back.

We look out on a farmer replanting
the rice-shoots one blade at a time.

You say that if it was up to you,
if poets could do long without cities,
or need other poets for more than tea or tobacco,

then you would live here in the flower forever.

iv. The Kinh Thầy Ferry

We think they are crossing.
Here where bombs fell under the cries of the stork,
where dike walls are alive with winter grasses.
We think they are crossing again.

On the slope where the pavement ends
and willows are thin arms in the wind,
a woman squats by her bicycle,
a rice bale strapped to its rack, too heavy to push.

We think they are crossing here,
just beyond the lotus growing in the bomb-crater ponds,
just beyond the ferry's dented bow,
our arms pushing with her now.

Huế, in Darkness

at Nam Giao Altar

I think sometimes Huế is the center of the universe,
    that thousands of eyes have turned toward us here.
The reticent eye of the full moon with clouds.
The burning eye of the lit bundle of incense
    wedged into stone.
The magnified eye of the imperial courtyard,
    its marble sounding board.
The skeptical eye
    of the woman praying on the shadowy steps.
The blinding eyes of the van's headlights.
    And the soft pinpoints of candles cradled on the river.
The eyes of the many no longer here.
    And the living eyes of friends who are.

V

Estuary

for William Stafford

i.

Early for the reading, I studied the statue
of Washington, sat on the stone sill, then
strolled the block with children on a school trip,
came back to sit with workers eating lunch.

When you began, you recalled waking to rain—
"old Northwestern friend"—pressed against
the high ridge of your hotel. You said it made
for a long guessing at what lay beyond:

roaring jets, trucks, unmuffled dumpsters
clanging, the hoot of river tugs, the city-din.
First to mind was not our almost fatal excess,
but delight in the hints of "our world breathing."

ii.

A dark wet gravel clinking underfoot.
A fledgling eagle in the spruce
indifferent but unable to let anything pass.
You opening the jalousie door, new work in hand,
the page flipping as if it were a salmon culled arching,
lifted up, out, still alive.

iii.

A tanager swayed on a gnarled
juniper and listened in,
but a small stone clicked down
and the bird fled, while we, mutable
in our flesh, shivered in the early snow.
Heavens over the Wasatch were

breaking into columns of light,
and without a word you started up
the scree, as if you knew the next place
we'd have to meet was at the top.

iv.

Among the fragrant juniper a continent away
there is a stream lively with steelhead.

I imagine you now, your wandering thought
making a small joining at the far reaches
with mine, just beyond our lines of sight,

where the jagged Point, strong emissary
of the land, goes gray with fog and gives
itself over to the ocean, the long-combers,

where, wave-scoured and almost invisible,
a cedar log rolls in on every one, then back.

St. John's Point

Donegal

After supper, we pedaled to a sandstone cove,
watched the tidepool dramas, the opal periwinkles,

waving sea lettuce, hermit crabs nibbling.
We wondered together what it might mean to depend

on the flat, warmed rocks slipping under the tide.
When we started back, it was pitch black everywhere,

and I asked if you'd ever heard of night vision,
how the iris will stretch to gather in ambient

light from stars, moon, and the distant city.
But there was none or little that night.

There was internment in the North, and imaginary
gunmen hiding in the ditches. A fine gravel

on the road made the wheels slip. On our faces
we could feel moisture from the ocean, hear

the thump of surf, and all the little mechanical
sounds of gear-teeth, sprockets, oily axles,

the squeak of saddle springs when we hit the ruts,
the metal of handlebars that sometimes touched.

Fragments on the Last Night

What would slip by stands
miraculously under the window,
hidden in a sentence, a phrase,
a ground fog lifting, or is it settling?

In a gravel wash, on a pale mossy
stalk of Great Mullein two goldfinches
grip, and the stalk sways like a wand.
It reminds me of breathing.

There are those who think the origin
of poetry is a deity. Others say it is
only a part of the self normally asleep.
Some will declare it is loss, that mortal

shale we all plummet toward.
Tonight I think it is more like breathing.
Like Whitman reciting poems
to the surf, aligning his rhythms,

like breathing. Like a day marked
by love for yourself and at least one
other, which is just like breathing,
only a little harder.

The Meadow

A friend spoke as if she thought I understood
something of her loss, and I pretended,
for reasons I cannot fathom, that I did,
and could say what would help her,
but that which came out
was kin to what we spit up after choking.

I said pain like this is a fire curtain we pass
through once and then we never feel quite
this way again. What I wanted to do
was open myself from sternum to throat,
pull out the organ of affection and learn
what it thought it had to teach.

In the meadow I see timbered logs,
the radiant centers of each, their knots,
their branches at the whorls. I see how
they bleed a silvery gum fragrant with age.

There is spring in the meadow, and it breeds
shapes which come and hover, round
ghostly presences, bleating sorry, very sorry.

That most innocent, indestructible of forms. . .

Lean-To

Into the dayroom long and polished as a bowling alley,
a nurse wheels in a tray with Dixie cups,
a few pills in each. The patients, none of them young,
and all women, are in varied states of psychosis
or stupor. Some are strapped at the wrist.
Others are belted at the chest to keep them upright.
An ebullient, gray-haired volunteer plays carols
and show tunes on a tiny harmonica.
"Who doesn't like music?" he asks us,
but my sister and I, we hardly notice.
The television is loudly on, the camera panning over
a banquet table, candles, the mound of the turkey,
a wainscot dining room. The camera cuts to another
part of the house where a lubricious interlude
has just finished. The actor is working at his Windsor knot
while she, in a slip, sits on the bed and brushes
her hair as if it were to blame.
(We grin. We sense we are going to like this part.)
He firmly declares, "I will *not* seek a divorce,"
and that his belief in family is unwavering,
despite what happened. She in the warm spirit
of the season says, "I understand, I knew what
I was getting into." Now it's back to the dining room
where someone murmurs "mouthwatering."
It is the moment the minister arrives.
We hope more illicit sex is in the offing,
and other forms of forgivable wickedness
we might have giggled over, years ago
when we sat together under a lean-to
we had made out of discarded Christmas trees.
It was then, while spruce needles fell on our hair,
she explained to me how male and female fit.

The sleet outside ticked so loudly on the icy sidewalk
we could hardly hear who was calling us in.
It was a voice which seemed as far away
from us as the nurse now blocking the TV,
who leans over and says, "It's your turn,
Mary Pat," and stays until she swallows.

The Raisin

Two slow laps on the path by the beach,
the two of us irritable, breathing hard,
petering out early, then walking under jets
on their low-angle approaches to Logan.
This week, my wife's mother will lose
her hair when the chemicals kick in.

I am thinking about molecules that brew
under the yew bark, and the three turbans
we ordered from a catalog whose models
had faces which looked much too fleshy,
much too happy, and not really bald.
When my father died, the nurse wrote "wasted"

on his chart. I thought she had been searching
for a word, but no, this was to say tumors
were eating sugar out of every cell in his body.
Out at the end of the breakwater, two fishermen
in waders stand at the foamy trace that empties
Pleasure Bay into the harbor. Seagulls

wheel overhead, their feathers clean, crisp.
On a trash-barrel rim, the grand sultan
of these birds perches and guards his food
with glossy dignity. Unmoved, impervious.
Meanwhile my wife wonders if the harbor
flounder are polluted. She goes on to tell me

about her visit to the Wellness Center where
the group leader gave her a raisin to hold, asking
her to feel its ridges and look deeply into it,
and think of the grape as a being composed
of the rain, sun, and soil that fed the vines.
I said, you should've eaten it, but she said

it looked to her like a tumor. Now we both
feel as if we are swimming through icy water,
the tide dragging us beyond the breakwater.
We're being held under for a long, airless stretch,
and when we come up, all we do is gasp
at the strange new being burning above us.

Corita's Tank

The freeway shudders under heavy trailers,
and layers of accumulating afternoon heat.
    A cormorant perches atop an inlet piling,
the creosote log, driven into the silt, swaying
    in a trace of tide. Desolate gravel raked
around the storage farms, the winter-fuel stockpile.
    Then, monumentally squat, the natural gas
tank, its white bulk painted with six rough stripes,
    each band of color an act of faith
to alter, however slightly, the public soul.

When the Vietnamese literary delegation
ate lunch with us under the founders' portraits,
    Hưu Thỉnh said that in Viet Nam no one felt
censored. Writing was for the "survival of the nation,"
    a selflessness asked of all, especially artists.
I was polite, but eager to tell him of the dissidence
    of Sister Corita, her profile of Hồ Chí Minh
on the gas tank. On the left side of the blue swath
    you can see the curve of his brow, the wisps
off his chin, with one eye gazing westward over
    this highway, surprised perhaps to be there.

I am sweating at the wheel, inching
forward, trying not to graze the man in a field jacket
    as he pushes a shopping cart down the inside
lane. I have seen him before, with his redeemable
    trash: the empties, a comforter. Some tap
their temples, call him a nut, but a sadness thick
    as heat off the freeway comes over me
when I picture him falling into fitful, dangerous sleep,
    or leaning to piss on the scored abutments.

Maybe it's allegiance mixed in with the sadness,
    an intuition that no matter how desolate
or bereft we become, there are signs of hidden life,
    weedy, rooted, and not apologetic.
He is barely audible in his discourse to no one,
    his lips just visible behind a slow,
deeply serious, upraised middle finger. The desire
    is to break anything, a face, a wall,
a window. It's a spirit mean as asphalt: pungent,
    pliable, staining, flattening.

    Maybe he's measuring off the stretch
of bay out to the island where they aerate the sludge.
    Or maybe he is just aiming at the jet
coming in, or planning to drop a mortar shell down
    an imaginary tube. Or he's keying on the glint,
the flare under the aluminum wings coming in over
    the art of Sister Corita, over Uncle Ho,
over the boiling line of stalled cars and mirror-glass
    towers of wealth which are blinking in code,
coming to rest here on the rim of a broken wheel,
    the hub of which this man thinks of as home.

Rows of Buddhas, Receding

at the Temple of Nguyễn Trãi (1380–1420)

Into the room of carved wooden
       statues, skin painted gold, robes
              a deep violet, sometimes

a saffron sash: three or four
       Buddhas across, rising and receding
              to the largest floating on a carved lotus,

an incense ring drifting back
       down the stepped rows,
              as if prayers it had carried had been

heard by past rectors
       and teachers, each in a guise
              or posture, curved fingers measuring

a magnitude at the center
       of a spinning, aortal wheel
              where nothing breathes, or sounds,

or is. Go past the funerary urns,
       guardians of the poet's sleep,
              his ashes scattered over pine

needles and clay which
       cling to the shoe while a deer
              somewhere above you,

with its nubbed, black horns,
       and its ears bailing the sweet air,
              lowers its muzzle to

a spring under rows of
        pines rising and receding
                upward, each a Buddha unto itself:

a teacher, a discipline,
        a silence composing the dream
                of each of us all over again.

Notes

"Tereus": The mythological Greek king, after raping and imprisoning his sister-in-law Philomel, cut her tongue out to prevent her from telling what had happened.

"The Alabaster Stork" and "Letter": According to Vietnamese legend, in times of great turmoil, a child poet will appear, one whose verses will guide and inspire. During the American War in Viet Nam, Trần Đăng Khoa was widely thought, among the then North Vietnamese, to be the child poet of the era.

"Harpagus": Advisor and kinsman to Astyages, King of Lydia. Astyages was the grandfather of Cyrus the Great. A prophecy warned that Astyages' grandson would replace him on the throne, so he ordered Harpagus to see that the infant was killed. Harpagus, however, saved the child and had him raised in a neighboring kingdom. When Astyages learned that the boy was alive, he had Harpagus' children murdered, roasted, and served to him at a banquet.

"The Collage House": Dr. Frank P. Olson, a researcher in biochemical warfare, was in all likelihood murdered in 1953 by operatives of the Central Intelligence Agency. It was made to appear that Olson had jumped to his death from a window in the Statler Hotel in Manhattan. This came ten days after the Agency had given him a surreptitious dose of LSD.

"Seven Tongues of God": The title is borrowed from an essay by Timothy Leary.

"Huế, in Darkness": Nam Giao Altar means "Where the King Worships Heaven and Earth." It is a slightly concave stone platform which serves to magnify the voices of those who stand at the center of it.

"Corita's Tank": A large natural gas tank overlooking Boston harbor. It is painted with a rainbow design by Sister Corita Kent.

"Rows of Buddhas, Receding": Nguyễn Trãi was the first major Vietnamese poet to write in the vernacular. He also led an armed resistance against Chinese imperial forces.

"The Pale" is dedicated to William Lopes; "Archives" to Kevin Bowen; "Bones to Hà Nội" to Ma Văn Kháng; "Inscription" to Pham Tiến Duật and Nguyễn Duy; "Delphi" to David Grene; "A Reading during Time of War" to Nguyễn Đúc Mau; "Full Moon Boat" to Võ Quê and the Perfume River Ensemble; "Huế, in Darkness" to Maxine Hong Kingston; "Corita's Tank" to James Carroll.

FRED MARCHANT is the author of *Tipping Point,* winner of the 1993 Washington Prize in Poetry. His poems, essays, and reviews have appeared in many newspapers, journals, and anthologies, including *AGNI, Harvard Review,* and *Ploughshares,* and he has received fellowships from the MacDowell, Ucross, and Yaddo Colonies. Marchant was one of the first Marine officers to be honorably discharged as a conscientious objector to the war in Viet Nam. He currently teaches English and directs the creative writing program at Suffolk University in Boston. He is also a teaching affiliate at the William Joiner Center for the Study of War and Social Consequences at the University of Massachusetts, Boston.

This book was designed by Donna Burch. It is set in VinaGara type by Stanton Publication Services, Inc., and manufactured by Bang Printing on acid-free paper.

Graywolf Press is a not-for-profit, independent press. The books we publish include poetry, literary fiction, and cultural criticism. We are less interested in best-sellers than in talented writers who display a freshness of voice coupled with a distinct vision. We believe these are the very qualities essential to shape a vital and diverse culture.

Thankfully, many of our readers feel the same way. They have shown this through their desire to buy books by Graywolf writers; they have told us this themselves through their e-mail notes and at author events; and they have reinforced their commitment by contributing financial support, in small amounts and in large amounts, and joining the "Friends of Graywolf."

If you enjoyed this book and wish to learn more about Graywolf Press, we invite you to ask your bookseller or librarian about further Graywolf titles; or to contact us for a free catalog; or to visit our award-winning web site that features information about our forthcoming books.

We would also like to invite you to consider joining the hundreds of individuals who are already "Friends of Graywolf" by contributing to our membership program. Individual donations of any size are significant to us: they tell us that you believe that the kind of publishing we do *matters*. Our web site gives you many more details about the benefits you will enjoy as a "Friend of Graywolf"; but if you do not have online access, we urge you to contact us for a copy of our membership brochure.

www.graywolfpress.org

Graywolf Press
2402 University Avenue, Suite 203
Saint Paul, MN 55114
Phone: (651) 641-0077
Fax: (651) 641-0036
E-mail: wolves@graywolfpress.org

Graywolf Press is dedicated to the creation and promotion of thoughtful and imaginative contemporary literature essential to a vital and diverse culture. For further information, visit us online at: www.graywolfpress.org.

Other Graywolf titles you might enjoy are:

Bewitched Playground by David Rivard

Some Ether by Nick Flynn

Domestic Work by Natasha Trethewey

Pastoral by Carl Phillips

The Way It Is: New & Selected Poems by William Stafford